This is for you,

Karsten Luke Piper,

once the little boy crying for friends,
now a man who knows the Friend who will never leave you nor forsake you.
May you grow ever more close to him and he ever more dear to you. –NP

To Noah and Nathan, with love. –GS

• • • • • • • • •

Also by Noël Piper:
Most of All, Jesus Loves You!

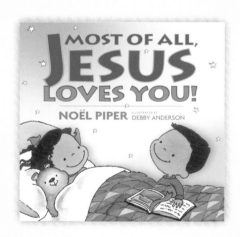

Do you want a FRIEND ?

Noël Piper

Illustrated by Gail Schoonmaker

CROSSWAY BOOKS • WHEATON, ILLINOIS

MOVING

One time there was a little boy. His family moved to a new place. He didn't know anyone in the houses nearby. That made him feel lonely.

So he sat on the front steps and cried out, "Friends! Frie-e-e-ends!" He wanted a friend.

Before long he found some
friends. Some of them were young.
Some of them were old.
And some were in between.

Do you want a friend too?

Do you want a friend who **loves** you?

[Nothing] will be able to separate us from the
love of God in Christ Jesus our Lord.

Romans 8:38–39

Do you want a friend who **comforts** you when you are sad or sick?

Through Christ we share abundantly in comfort.

2 Corinthians 1:5

Do you want a friend who helps you be **Strong?**

I can do all things through him [Jesus, the Lord] who strengthens me. Philippians 4:13

Do you want a friend who wants to **be with** you?

I will never leave you
nor forsake you.

Hebrews 13:5

Do you want a friend who helps you **know** God?

I have called you friends, for all that I have heard from my Father I have made known to you.

John 15:15

Do you want a friend
who **prays** for you?

Jesus . . . lifted up his eyes to heaven, and said, . . . "I am praying for them. I am not praying for the world but for those whom you have given me, for they are yours." John 17:1, 9

Do you want a friend who
makes you **happy?**

[Jesus said,] "These things I have spoken to you, that my joy may be in you, and that your joy may be full." John 15:11

o you want a friend who **forgives** you when you do something wrong?

In him we have redemption through his blood, the forgiveness of our trespasses, according to the riches of his grace. Ephesians 1:7

Do you want a friend wh
helps you do **good**?

We are his workmanship, created in Christ Jesus
for good works, which God prepared beforehand, that we
should walk in them. Ephesians 2:10

o you want a friend who will **save** you from danger?

You shall call his name Jesus, for he will save his people from their sins.

Matthew 1:21

Maybe you have a lot of friends.
But can any of them do ALL
these things ALL the time? No.
Jesus is the only friend who
is everything we need.
There is no friend like Jesus.

May the God of peace . . . equip you with everything good that you may do his will, working in us that which is pleasing in his sight, through Jesus Christ, to whom be glory forever and ever.

Hebrews 13:20–21

But we do so many bad things.
How can we have a friend who is so good?
How can Jesus be our friend? The answer is that Jesus
died for sinners. Then he rose from the dead. Jesus can be
a great friend because he is a great Savior.

Greater love has no one than this, that someone lay
down his life for his friends. John 15:13

Jesus is the best friend of all!

For God so loved the world, that he gave his only Son, that whoever believes in him should not perish but have eternal life. John 3:16

One There Is, Above All Others

John Newton

Anton Peter Berggreen

One there is, a - bove all oth - ers, Well de -
serves the name of Friend; His is love be - yond a
broth - er's, Cost - ly, free, and knows no
end. They who once His kind - ness
prove Find it ev - er - last - ing love.

2. Which of all our friends to save us,
Could or would have shed their blood?
But our Jesus died to have us
Reconciled, in Him to God:
This was boundless love indeed!
Jesus is a Friend in need.

3. When He lived on earth abasèd,
Friend of sinners was His name;
Now, above all glory raisèd,
He rejoices in the same:
Still He calls them brethren, friends,
And to all their wants attends.

4. O for grace our hearts to soften!
Teach us, Lord, at length to love;
We, alas! forget too often,
What a Friend we have above:
But when home our souls are broug
We will love Thee as we ought.

Do You Want a Friend?
Text copyright © 2009 by Noël Piper
Illustrations copyright © 2009 by Gail Schoonmaker
Published by Crossway Books
        a publishing ministry of Good News Publishers
        1300 Crescent Street, Wheaton, Illinois 60187

Cover design: Amy Bristow
Cover illustration: Gail Schoonmaker
First printing 2009
Printed in U.S.A.

Scripture quotations are from the ESV® Bible (*The Holy Bible, English Standard Version*®), copyright © 2001 by Crossway Bibles, a publishing ministry of Good News Publishers. Used by permission. All rights reserved.

Hardcover ISBN: 978-4335-0621-5
PDF ISBN: 978-1-4335-0622-2
Mobipocket ISBN: 978-4335-0623-9

Library of Congress Cataloging-in-Publication Data
Piper, Noël, 1947-
  Do You Want a Friend? / Noël Piper ; illustrated by Gail Schoonmaker.
    p. cm.
  ISBN 978-1-4335-0621-5 (hc)
  1. Friendship--Religious aspects--Christianity--Juvenile literature. I. Schoonmaker, Gail. II. Title.

BV4647.F7P57 2009
241'.6762--dc22   #26289/609   2008043042

L B	17	16	15	14	13	12	11	10	09
14	13	12	11	10	9	8	7	6	5	4	3	2	1

Additional resources from Noël and her husband John
—including many free downloads of books, articles, and
audio—may be found at www.desiringGOD.org.
Desiring God Ministries—1-888-346-4700 (toll-free)